Pebble® Plus

BIRDS OF PREY

California CONDORS

by Mary R. Dunn

Consulting Editor: Gail Saunders-Smith, PhD

Consultant: Cynthia Stringfield, DMV
Professor and Chair/Veterinarian,
Moorpark College, Moorpark, California

CAPSTONE PRESS
a capstone imprint

Pebble Plus is published by Capstone Press,
1710 Roe Crest Drive, North Mankato, Minnesota 56003
www.capstonepub.com

Library of Congress Cataloging-in-Publication Data
Dunn, Mary R.
California condors / by Mary R. Dunn
pages. cm.—(Pebble Plus. Birds of Prey)
Includes bibliographical references and index.
Summary: "Describes the characteristics, habitat, behavior, life cycle, and
threats to California condors"—Provided by publisher.
Audience: Ages 5-8
Audience: Grades K to 3.
ISBN 978-1-4914-2089-8 (library binding)
ISBN 978-1-4914-2307-3 (paperback)
ISBN 978-1-4914-2330-1 (eBook PDF)
1. California condor—Juvenile literature. I. Title.
598.92—dc23

2014032767

Editorial Credits
Jeni Wittrock, editor; Peggie Carley and Janet Kusmierski, designers;
Svetlana Zhurkin, media researcher; Katy LaVigne, production specialist

Photo Credits
Alamy: Q-Images, 17, Rachel Wright, 19; AP Photo: National Park Service/Gavin
Emmonds, 15; Dreamstime: Michael Elliott, cover, back cover, 1, 7; Getty Images:
Adam Jones, 9, John Cancalosi, 21, Quincy Dein, 13, Tim Laman, 11;
Minden Pictures: Yva Momatiuk & John Eastcott, 5; Shutterstock: balounm,
back cover (background)

Note to Parents and Teachers

The Birds of Prey set supports national science standards related to
life science. This book describes and illustrates California condors.
The images support early readers in understanding the text. The
repetition of words and phrases helps early readers learn new
words. This book also introduces early readers to subject-specific
vocabulary words, which are defined in the Glossary section. Early
readers may need assistance to read some words and to use the
Table of Contents, Glossary, Read More, Internet Sites, Critical
Thinking with the Common Core, and Index sections of the book.

Printed in the United States of America in Stevens Point, Wisconsin
102014   008479WZS15

Table of Contents

High Fliers

A California condor swoops
through the sky. His big wings
only have to flap a little.
The condor lands on a cliff
to rest in the sun.

Scientists put numbers on California condors
to help track the birds.

Up Close

Black and white feathers cover California condors' bodies. They have bald pink heads and red eyes. Male and female condors look the same.

California condors are the largest North American bird. They weigh about 22 pounds (10 kilograms). Their wings are about 10 feet (3 meters) wide.

Condor Homes

Southwest United States and Baja California in Mexico are home to California condors. They build nests in hillside caves or in tall trees.

California Condor Range

where california condors live

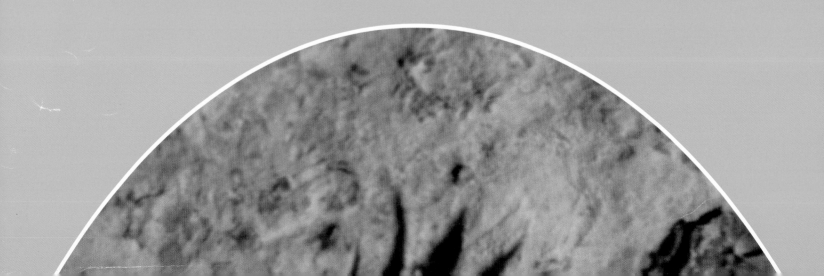

Mealtime

California condors are scavengers. They look for food while flying. Their eyes easily spot dead deer, cattle, or sea lions far below.

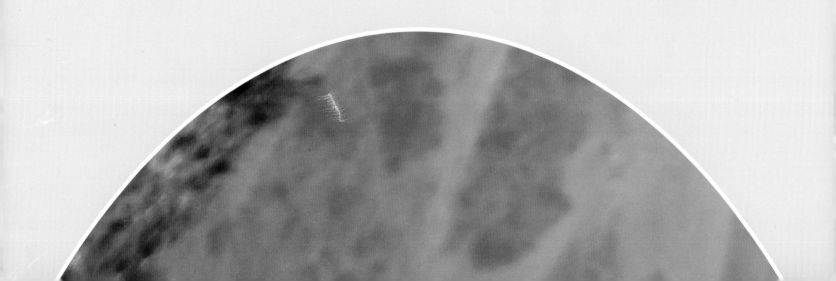

Condor Families

Female condors lay one white egg every other year. The egg hatches in about 56 days. Both parents feed the chick and keep it warm.

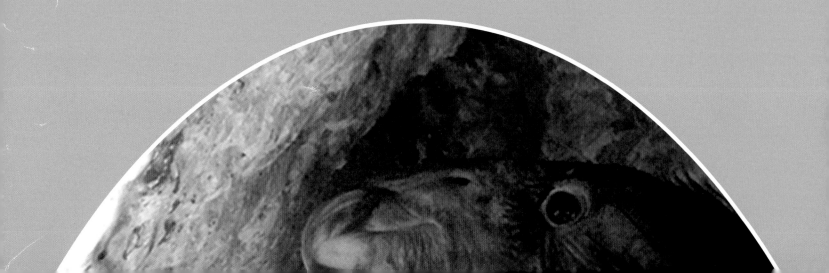

Fluffy gray chicks leave the nest after about three months. But they stay near their parents. The chicks can fly after six or seven months.

In Danger

Hiss! Condors warn enemies to keep away. People are condors' worst enemies. They destroy the birds' homes and pollute condors' food.

Only around 400 California condors are still alive. Scientists work hard to save these endangered birds. Safe, healthy condors can live 45 years.

Glossary

bald—without hair, fur, or feathers

chick—a young bird

destroy—to tear down or wreck

endangered—in danger of dying out

flap—to move wings up and down to fly

hillside—found on the side of a hill

pollute—to make something dirty or unsafe

scavenger—an animal that feeds on animals that are already dead

swoop—to fly in a smooth, easy curve

Read More

Boothroyd, Jennifer. *Endangered and Extinct Birds.* Animals in Danger. Minneapolis: Lerner Pub., 2014.

Curtis, Jennifer Keats. *Raptor Centers.* Animal Helpers. Mount Pleasant, S.C.: Arbordale Publishing, 2014.

Dunn, Mary R. *Turkey Vultures.* Birds of Prey. North Mankato, Minn.: Capstone Press, 2015.

Internet Sites

FactHound offers a safe, fun way to find Internet sites related to this book. All of the sites on FactHound have been researched by our staff.

Here's all you do:

Visit *www.facthound.com*

Type in this code: 9781491420898

Check out projects, games and lots more at
www.capstonekids.com

Critical Thinking Using the Common Core

Condors eat animals that are already dead. What might happen to a condor that eats prey that died from poison? (Integration of Knowledge and Ideas)

Reread pages 14 and 16. Describe how condors raise their chicks. (Key Ideas and Details)

Index

Word Count: 213
Grade: 1
Early-Intervention Level: 14